MW01167382

The ABCs of Self-Esteem

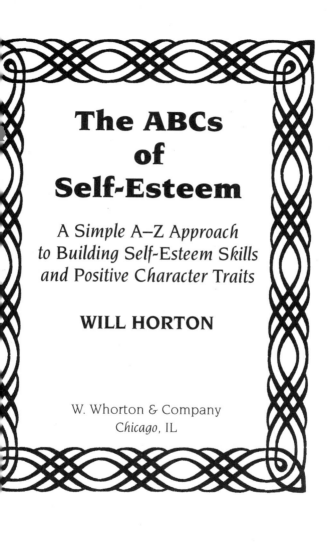

The ABCs
of
Self-Esteem

A Simple A–Z Approach
to Building Self-Esteem Skills
and Positive Character Traits

WILL HORTON

W. Whorton & Company
Chicago, IL

Library of Congress Cataloging-in-Publication data is found on last page of this book.

To my son, Will Horton, Jr.—
I am proud of you.

Contents

INTRODUCTION

The ABCs of Self-Esteem uses a simple A–Z theme approach to building self-esteem, which helps children develop highly effective habits and character traits that will lead to responsible citizenship, happiness, and success in life; in short, a character ethos.

This book was designed to be used by families. Parents can use *The ABCs of Self-Esteem* to enhance and reinforce their own self-esteem skills—skills that have already been developed but may have become dormant over the years.

As their children's first and most influential teacher, parents can use this book to help their children build self-esteem and positive character traits. As children grow and develop, their self-concept will change and evolve. Children need high self-esteem and a positive self-concept to help mitigate against any negative influences they may encounter while growing up.

The ABCs of Self-Esteem can be learned best by choosing a weekly theme, such as attitude. Discuss the theme as a family. For school-age children they should learn the word and its meaning and write the word. This helps build their vocabulary. The weekly theme activities help children develop language arts skills. See the Activity Guide in the back of the book for more details.

The ABCs of Self-Esteem uses a mnemonic technique to building self-esteem and positive character traits. Mnemonics is a technique parents can use to help improve their children's memory. For example, the first self-esteem theme is attitude—"A is for attitude." Children will associate the code letter *A* to the new word and to the theme *attitude*. The following themes are used in this book.

1. Attitude
2. Best
3. Can

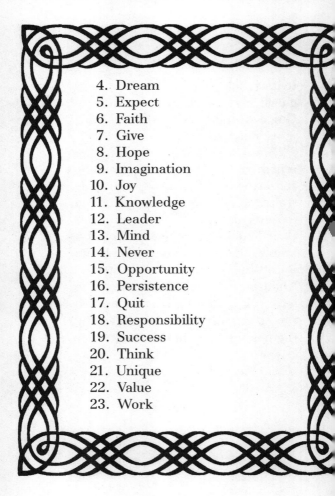

24. The Unknown
25. Yes
26. Zeal

Spend as much time as your children need on each theme in order to master each concept. Once all themes have been completed and all of the concepts mastered, the process can be repeated. This helps to establish the concepts firmly in your children's memory. Pick out favorite themes and review those as needed.

You may decide that you want to substitute or add new themes. Please feel free to do so. Or you may decide that you do not want to use any of the themes and develop your own. Again, this is your prerogative. Do whatever works best for you and your children. If you decide to make changes or have suggestions, write or e-mail me at the address located in the back of this book.

Each theme is designed to teach positive self-esteem, positive self-expectancy, positive character traits, and self-determination. Children are our future, and the state of their minds will determine the direction of their future and that of our world. In order to become successful in life, children need to have faith, hope, and confidence in their abilities to compete and succeed in our new global society. When children have high self-esteem and believe in themselves they become more enthusiastic about learning and learn more. It does not matter whether your child wants to be a lawyer, doctor, mechanic, teacher, or computer operator; the need for learning never stops in our technologically driven society.

Positive self-esteem and positive character traits are interconnected; they have a synergist relationship. When they are developed as a unit in children, the children develop completely; that is, the children grow up to be people who are happy, intelligent, and socially and emotionally well-balanced.

Dr. Martin Luther King, Jr. said: "The function of education, therefore, is to teach one to think intensively and to think critically. But education which stops with efficiency may prove the greatest menace to society. The most dangerous criminal may be the man gifted with reason, but with no morals." The words of Theodore Roosevelt echo King's teaching: "To educate a man in mind and not in morals is to educate a menace to society."

The development of character ethos, taught in *The ABCs of Self-Esteem,* are the basic foundational values and principles to live by, which will guide children to a life of happiness, self-fulfillment, and success. Children, as well as adults, need to continually upgrade their skills to meet the challenges for professional success. When children are expected to learn and succeed, they learn more and are more successful. Marian Wright Edelman says, "Don't ever stop learning and improving your mind or you're going to be left behind. The world is changing like a kaleidoscope right before our eyes."

The former president of Morehouse College and a mentor to Dr. Martin Luther King, Jr., Dr. Benjamin E. Mays teaches: "You are what you aspire to be, and not what you now are; you are what you do with your mind, and you are what you do with your youth." Mays' eloquent wisdom continues: "It is not your environment, it is

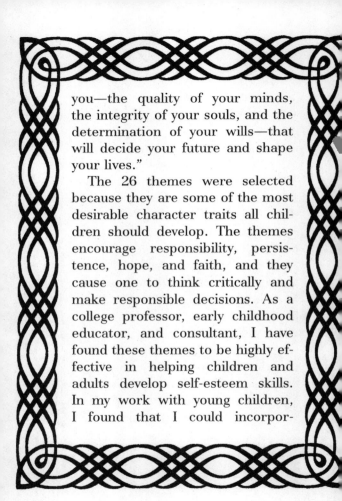

you—the quality of your minds, the integrity of your souls, and the determination of your wills—that will decide your future and shape your lives."

The 26 themes were selected because they are some of the most desirable character traits all children should develop. The themes encourage responsibility, persistence, hope, and faith, and they cause one to think critically and make responsible decisions. As a college professor, early childhood educator, and consultant, I have found these themes to be highly effective in helping children and adults develop self-esteem skills. In my work with young children, I found that I could incorporate character-building skills with the development of positive self-esteem.

In this short but powerful book, which includes a wealth of information and techniques for success, one of my major challenges was deciding which individuals and/or quotations best represented the themes. I wanted to quote individuals who had a demonstrated record of positive self-esteem. Such individuals include the following:

- **Erich Fromm** (1900–1980) was a German-born American psychoanalyst and philosopher. Fromm believed, as I do, that human behavior is a

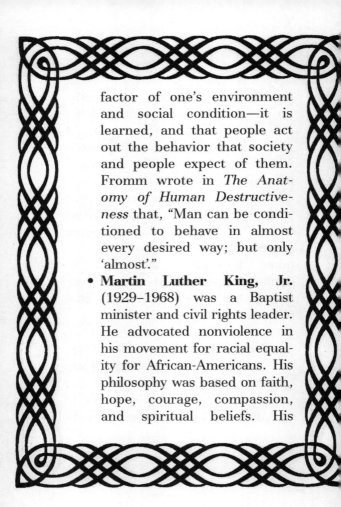

factor of one's environment and social condition—it is learned, and that people act out the behavior that society and people expect of them. Fromm wrote in *The Anatomy of Human Destructiveness* that, "Man can be conditioned to behave in almost every desired way; but only 'almost'."

- **Martin Luther King, Jr.** (1929–1968) was a Baptist minister and civil rights leader. He advocated nonviolence in his movement for racial equality for African-Americans. His philosophy was based on faith, hope, courage, compassion, and spiritual beliefs. His teachings were well-received by both African-Americans and whites, and he became a national leader and Nobel Peace Prize winner. Even though King believed in nonviolence, violence was usually used against him. King said, "The ultimate measure of a man is not where he stands in moments of comfort and convenience, but where he stands at times of challenge and controversy."

- **Franklin Delano Roosevelt** (1882–1945) was crippled by polio at the age of 39 but he refused to give up his dream of public service. He was elected president of the United States

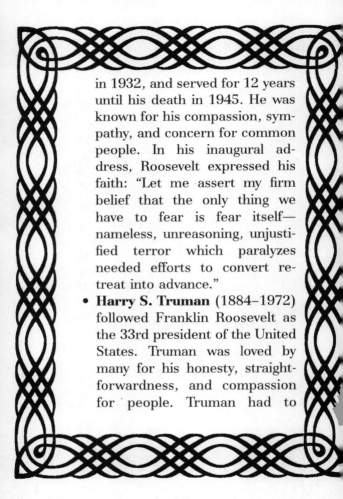

in 1932, and served for 12 years until his death in 1945. He was known for his compassion, sympathy, and concern for common people. In his inaugural address, Roosevelt expressed his faith: "Let me assert my firm belief that the only thing we have to fear is fear itself—nameless, unreasoning, unjustified terror which paralyzes needed efforts to convert retreat into advance."

- **Harry S. Truman** (1884–1972) followed Franklin Roosevelt as the 33rd president of the United States. Truman was loved by many for his honesty, straightforwardness, and compassion for people. Truman had to make critical decisions that displayed courage, creativity, and determination. He was not afraid of challenges and had enthusiasm and a will to win. The motto on his desk in The White House stated, "The buck stops here." The following quotation in *Mr. Citizen* illustrates Truman's attitude about challenges and decisions.

There has been a lot of talk lately about the burdens of the Presidency. Decisions that the President has to make often affect the lives of tens of millions of people around the world, but that does not mean

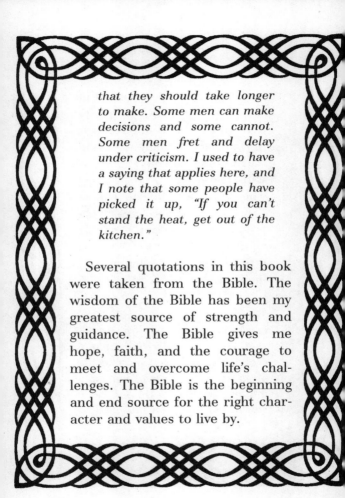

*that they should take longer
to make. Some men can make
decisions and some cannot.
Some men fret and delay
under criticism. I used to have
a saying that applies here, and
I note that some people have
picked it up, "If you can't
stand the heat, get out of the
kitchen."*

Several quotations in this book
were taken from the Bible. The
wisdom of the Bible has been my
greatest source of strength and
guidance. The Bible gives me
hope, faith, and the courage to
meet and overcome life's challenges. The Bible is the beginning
and end source for the right character and values to live by.

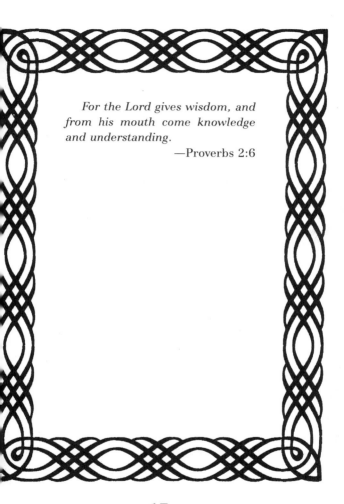

For the Lord gives wisdom, and from his mouth come knowledge and understanding.

—Proverbs 2:6

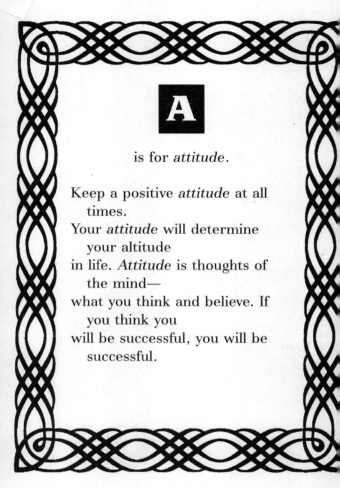

A

is for *attitude*.

Keep a positive *attitude* at all times.
Your *attitude* will determine your altitude
in life. *Attitude* is thoughts of the mind—
what you think and believe. If you think you
will be successful, you will be successful.

ATTITUDE

It is not important who you are or where you are at this stage of your life. What's important is your attitude about life. Your attitude acts as an agent of change; what you become depends on your attitude.

—Will Horton

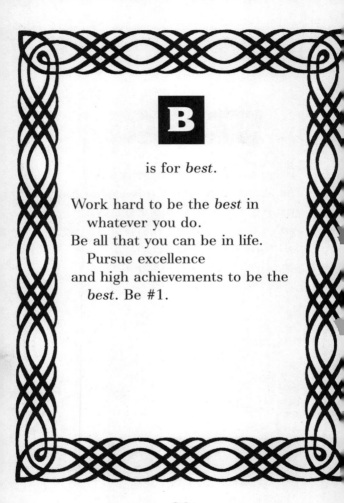

B

is for *best*.

Work hard to be the *best* in
whatever you do.
Be all that you can be in life.
Pursue excellence
and high achievements to be the
best. Be #1.

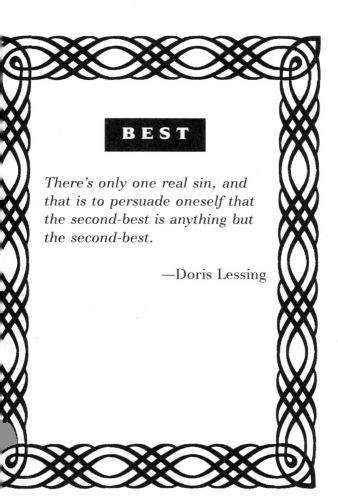

BEST

There's only one real sin, and that is to persuade oneself that the second-best is anything but the second-best.

—Doris Lessing

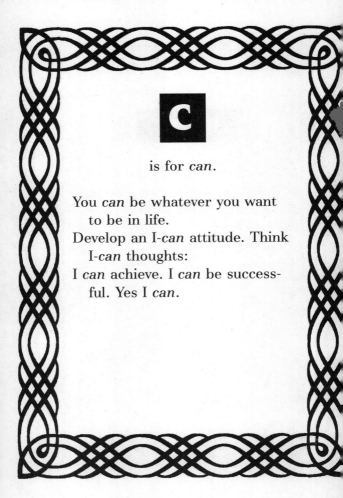

C

is for *can*.

You *can* be whatever you want
to be in life.
Develop an I-*can* attitude. Think
I-*can* thoughts:
I *can* achieve. I *can* be success-
ful. Yes I *can*.

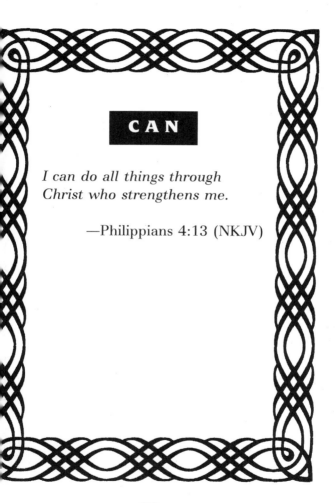

CAN

I can do all things through Christ who strengthens me.

—Philippians 4:13 (NKJV)

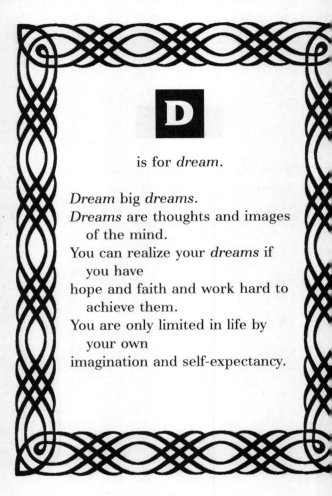

D

is for *dream*.

Dream big *dreams*.
Dreams are thoughts and images
   of the mind.
You can realize your *dreams* if
   you have
hope and faith and work hard to
   achieve them.
You are only limited in life by
   your own
imagination and self-expectancy.

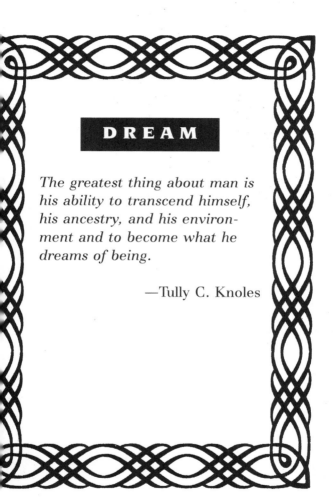

DREAM

The greatest thing about man is his ability to transcend himself, his ancestry, and his environment and to become what he dreams of being.

—Tully C. Knoles

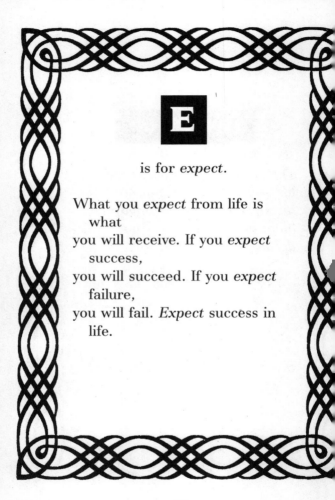

E

is for *expect*.

What you *expect* from life is what
you will receive. If you *expect* success,
you will succeed. If you *expect* failure,
you will fail. *Expect* success in life.

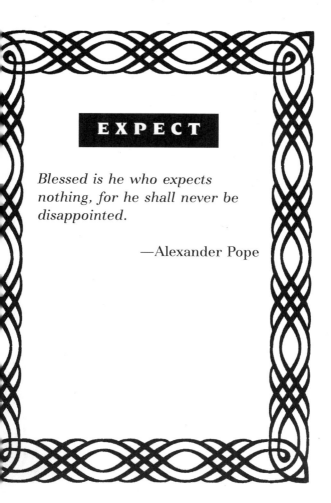

EXPECT

Blessed is he who expects nothing, for he shall never be disappointed.

—Alexander Pope

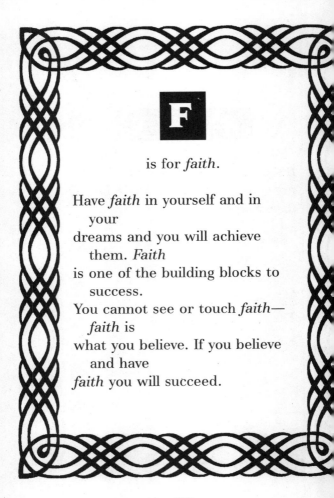

F

is for *faith*.

Have *faith* in yourself and in your
dreams and you will achieve them. *Faith*
is one of the building blocks to success.
You cannot see or touch *faith*—*faith* is
what you believe. If you believe and have
faith you will succeed.

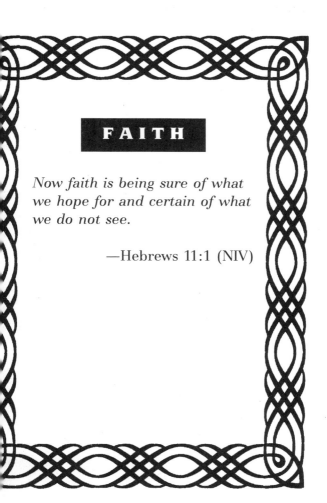

FAITH

Now faith is being sure of what we hope for and certain of what we do not see.

—Hebrews 11:1 (NIV)

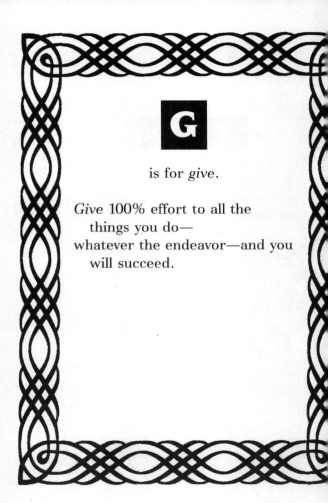

G

is for *give*.

Give 100% effort to all the
   things you do—
whatever the endeavor—and you
   will succeed.

GIVE

If a man is called to be a street sweeper, he should sweep streets even as Michelangelo painted, or Beethoven composed music, or Shakespeare wrote poetry. He should sweep streets so well that all the hosts of heaven and earth will pause to say, here lived a great street sweeper who did his job well.

—Martin Luther King, Jr.

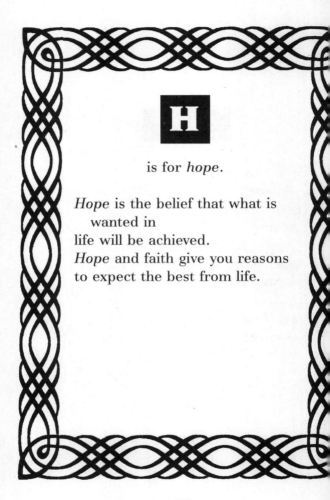

H

is for *hope*.

Hope is the belief that what is
    wanted in
life will be achieved.
Hope and faith give you reasons
to expect the best from life.

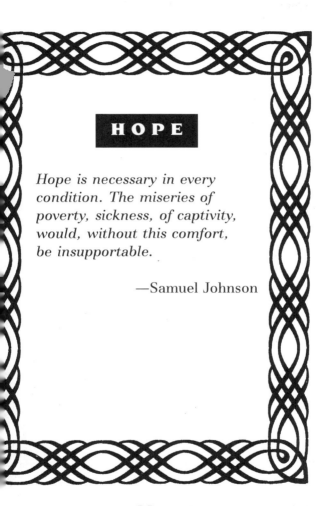

HOPE

Hope is necessary in every condition. The miseries of poverty, sickness, of captivity, would, without this comfort, be insupportable.

—Samuel Johnson

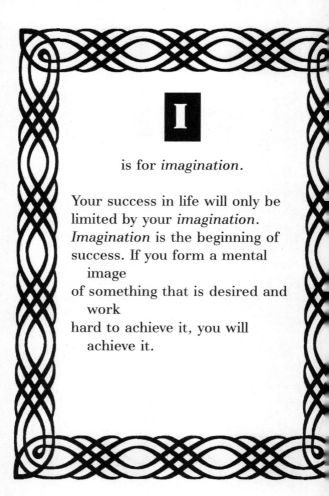

I

is for *imagination*.

Your success in life will only be
limited by your *imagination*.
Imagination is the beginning of
success. If you form a mental
 image
of something that is desired and
 work
hard to achieve it, you will
 achieve it.

IMAGINATION

*A man who has no imagination
has no wings.*

—Muhammad Ali

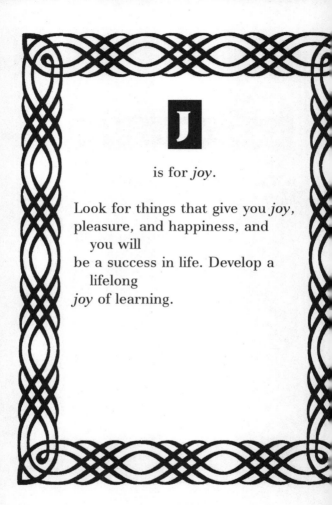

J

is for *joy*.

Look for things that give you *joy*,
pleasure, and happiness, and
    you will
be a success in life. Develop a
    lifelong
joy of learning.

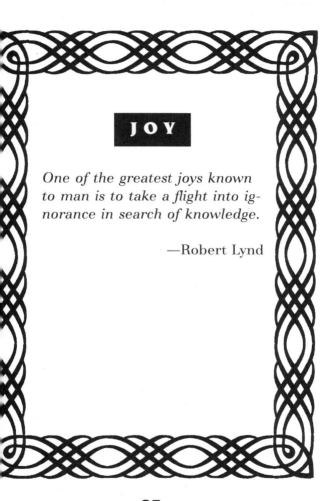

JOY

One of the greatest joys known to man is to take a flight into ignorance in search of knowledge.

—Robert Lynd

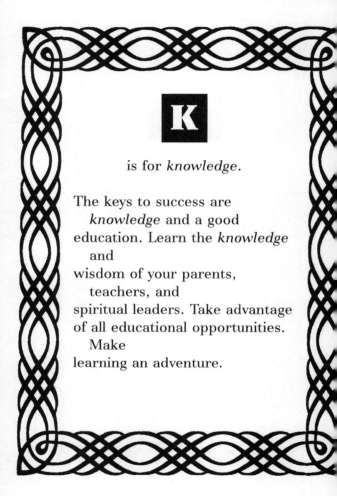

K

is for *knowledge*.

The keys to success are
  knowledge and a good
education. Learn the *knowledge*
  and
wisdom of your parents,
  teachers, and
spiritual leaders. Take advantage
of all educational opportunities.
  Make
learning an adventure.

KNOWLEDGE

*A wise man has great power,
and a man of knowledge in-
creases strength.*

—Proverbs 24:5 (NIV)

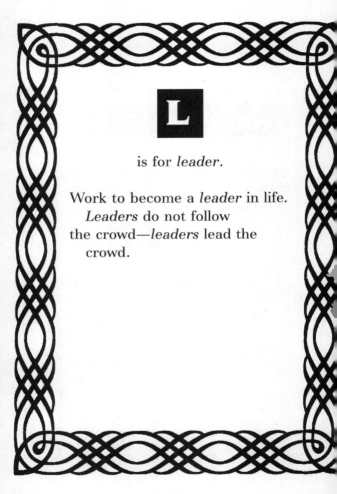

L

is for *leader*.

Work to become a *leader* in life.
Leaders do not follow
the crowd—*leaders* lead the
crowd.

LEADER

*Leaders see problems as oppor-
tunities. Leaders are able to
overcome problems by finding
a path that leads to success.
Leaders find a way to make
problems smaller and more
manageable by standing up to
them, or by going over or
around them.*

—Will Horton

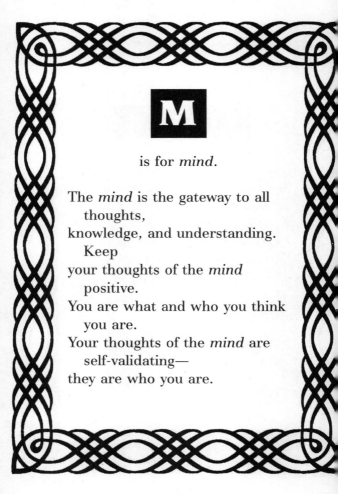

M

is for *mind*.

The *mind* is the gateway to all
   thoughts,
knowledge, and understanding.
   Keep
your thoughts of the *mind*
   positive.
You are what and who you think
   you are.
Your thoughts of the *mind* are
   self-validating—
they are who you are.

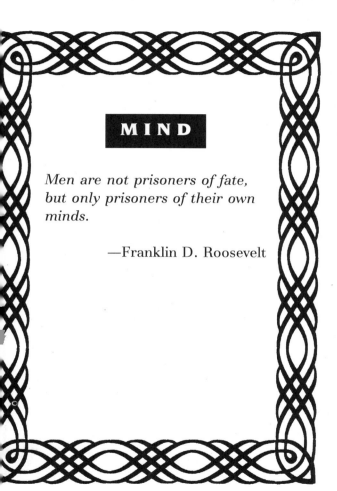

MIND

Men are not prisoners of fate,
but only prisoners of their own
minds.

—Franklin D. Roosevelt

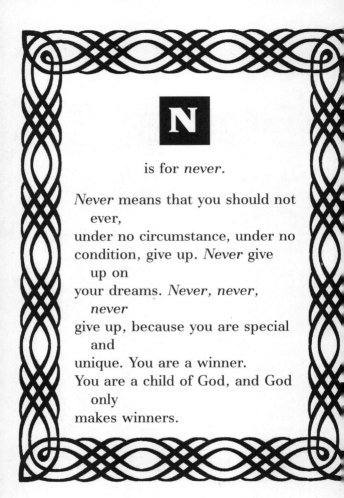

N

is for *never*.

Never means that you should not
    ever,
under no circumstance, under no
condition, give up. *Never* give
    up on
your dreams. *Never, never,
    never*
give up, because you are special
    and
unique. You are a winner.
You are a child of God, and God
    only
makes winners.

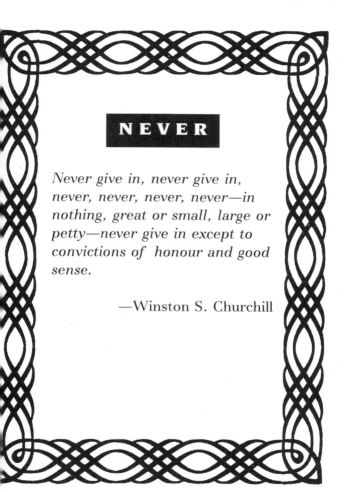

NEVER

Never give in, never give in, never, never, never, never—in nothing, great or small, large or petty—never give in except to convictions of honour and good sense.

—Winston S. Churchill

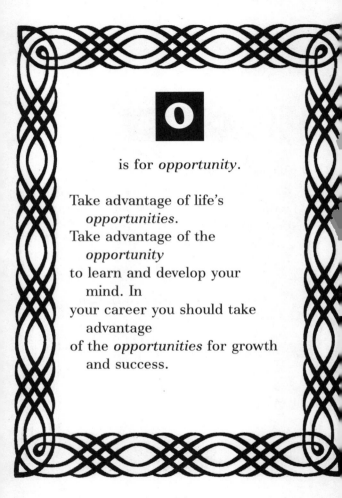

O

is for *opportunity*.

Take advantage of life's
 opportunities.
Take advantage of the
 opportunity
to learn and develop your
 mind. In
your career you should take
 advantage
of the *opportunities* for growth
 and success.

OPPORTUNITY

*The great secret of success in
life is for a man to be ready
when his opportunity comes.*

—Benjamin Disraeli

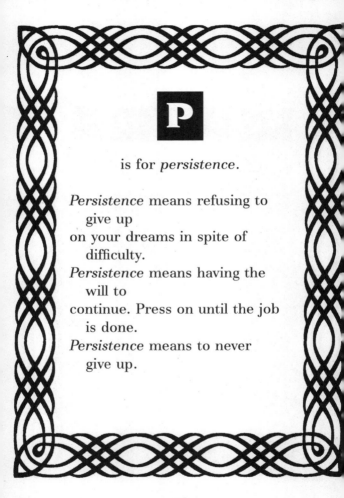

P

is for *persistence*.

Persistence means refusing to
    give up
on your dreams in spite of
    difficulty.
Persistence means having the
    will to
continue. Press on until the job
    is done.
Persistence means to never
    give up.

PERSISTENCE

Nothing is the World can take the place of persistence. Talent will not; nothing is more common than unsuccessful men with talent. Genius will not; unrewarded genius is almost a proverb. Education will not; the world is full of educated derelicts. Persistence and determination are omnipotent.

—Calvin Coolidge

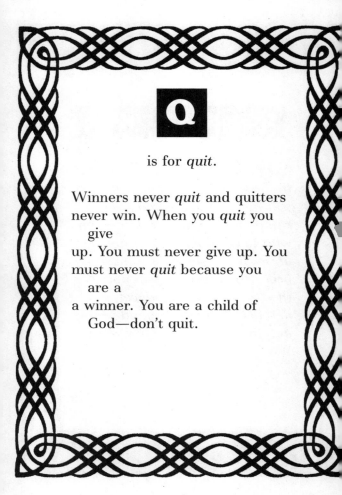

Q

is for *quit*.

Winners never *quit* and quitters
never win. When you *quit* you
  give
up. You must never give up. You
must never *quit* because you
  are a
a winner. You are a child of
  God—don't quit.

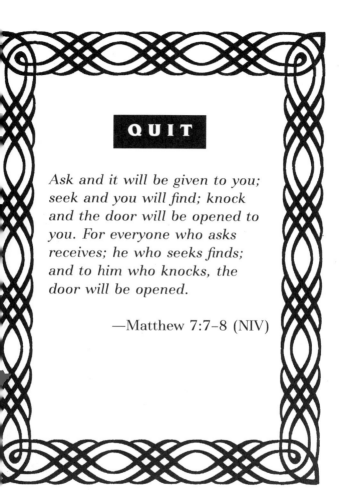

QUIT

Ask and it will be given to you; seek and you will find; knock and the door will be opened to you. For everyone who asks receives; he who seeks finds; and to him who knocks, the door will be opened.

—Matthew 7:7–8 (NIV)

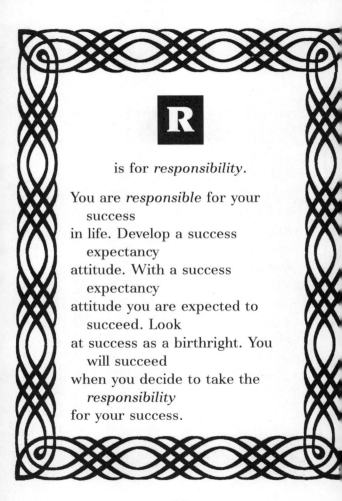

R

is for *responsibility*.

You are *responsible* for your
  success
in life. Develop a success
  expectancy
attitude. With a success
  expectancy
attitude you are expected to
  succeed. Look
at success as a birthright. You
  will succeed
when you decide to take the
  responsibility
for your success.

RESPONSIBILITY

When a man decides to do something, he must go all the way, but he must take responsibility for what he does. He must know first why he is doing it and then must proceed with his actions with no doubts or remorse.

—Carlos Castaneda

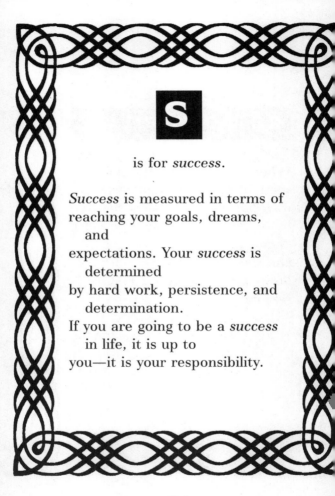

S

is for *success*.

Success is measured in terms of
reaching your goals, dreams,
   and
expectations. Your *success* is
   determined
by hard work, persistence, and
   determination.
If you are going to be a *success*
   in life, it is up to
you—it is your responsibility.

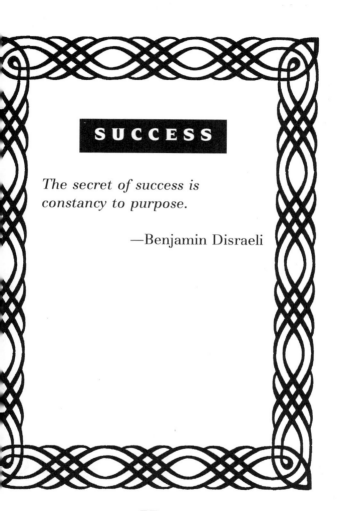

SUCCESS

*The secret of success is
constancy to purpose.*

—Benjamin Disraeli

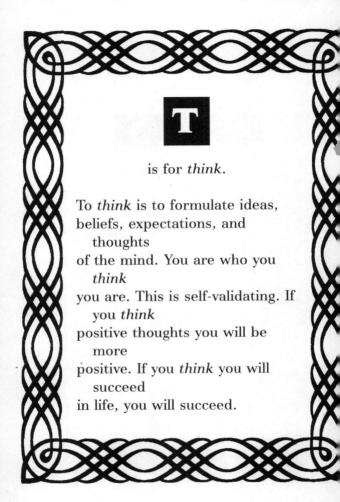

T

is for *think*.

To *think* is to formulate ideas,
beliefs, expectations, and
    thoughts
of the mind. You are who you
    think
you are. This is self-validating. If
    you *think*
positive thoughts you will be
    more
positive. If you *think* you will
    succeed
in life, you will succeed.

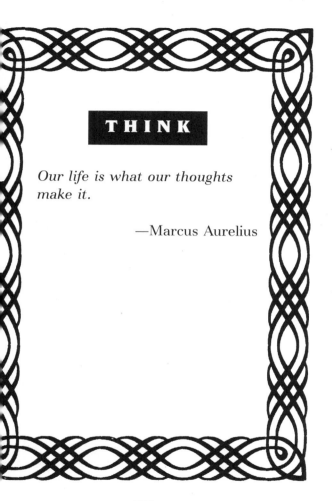

THINK

Our life is what our thoughts make it.

—Marcus Aurelius

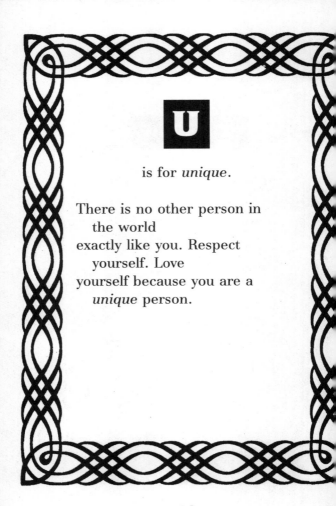

U

is for *unique*.

There is no other person in
   the world
exactly like you. Respect
   yourself. Love
yourself because you are a
   unique person.

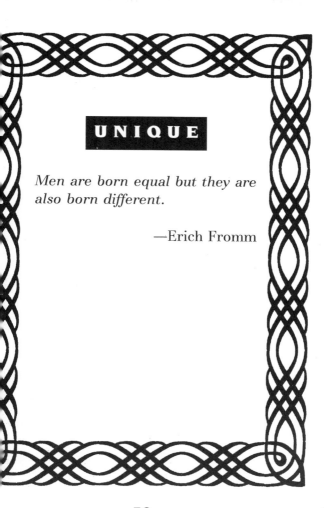

UNIQUE

*Men are born equal but they are
also born different.*

—Erich Fromm

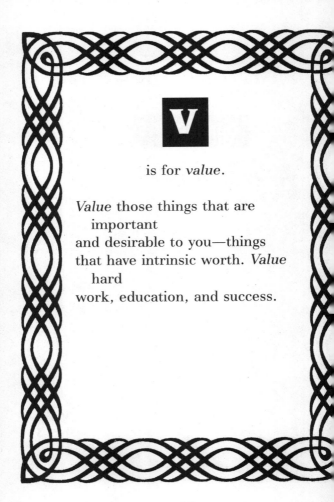

V

is for *value*.

Value those things that are
   important
and desirable to you—things
that have intrinsic worth. *Value*
   hard
work, education, and success.

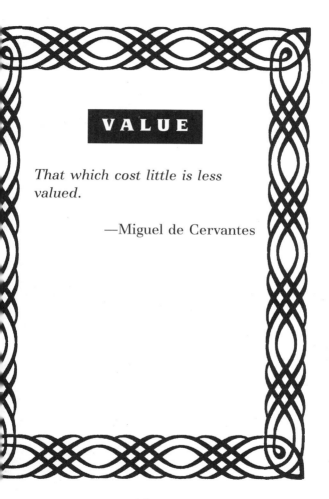

VALUE

That which cost little is less valued.

—Miguel de Cervantes

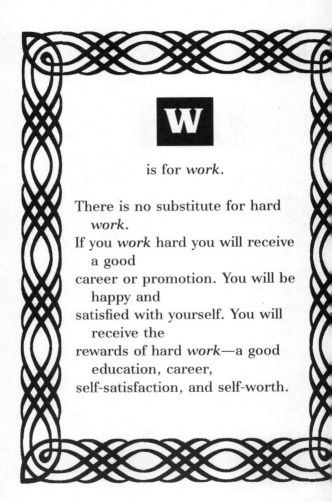

W

is for *work*.

There is no substitute for hard *work*.
If you *work* hard you will receive a good
career or promotion. You will be happy and
satisfied with yourself. You will receive the
rewards of hard *work*—a good education, career,
self-satisfaction, and self-worth.

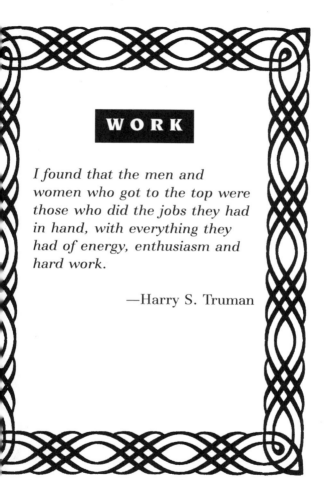

WORK

I found that the men and women who got to the top were those who did the jobs they had in hand, with everything they had of energy, enthusiasm and hard work.

—Harry S. Truman

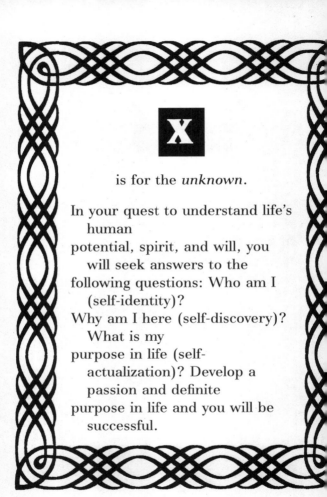

X

is for the *unknown*.

In your quest to understand life's human
potential, spirit, and will, you will seek answers to the
following questions: Who am I (self-identity)?
Why am I here (self-discovery)? What is my
purpose in life (self-actualization)? Develop a passion and definite
purpose in life and you will be successful.

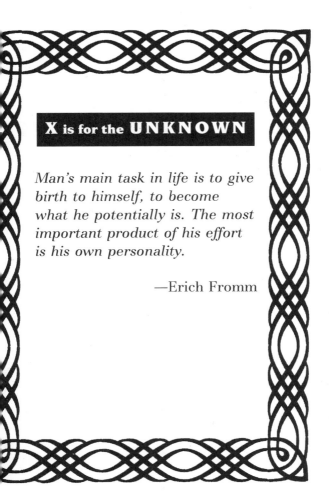

X is for the UNKNOWN

Man's main task in life is to give birth to himself, to become what he potentially is. The most important product of his effort is his own personality.

—Erich Fromm

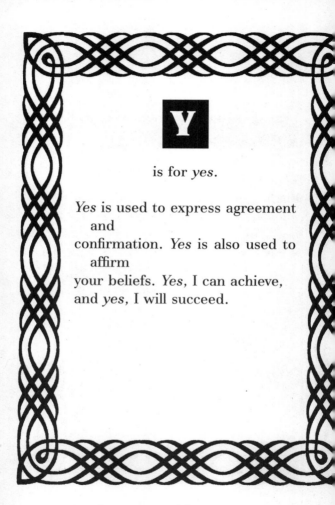

Y

is for *yes*.

Yes is used to express agreement and
confirmation. *Yes* is also used to affirm
your beliefs. *Yes*, I can achieve, and *yes*, I will succeed.

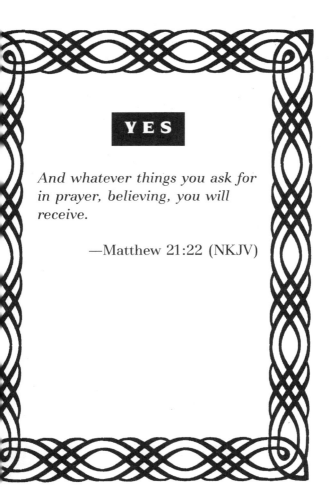

YES

And whatever things you ask for in prayer, believing, you will receive.

—Matthew 21:22 (NKJV)

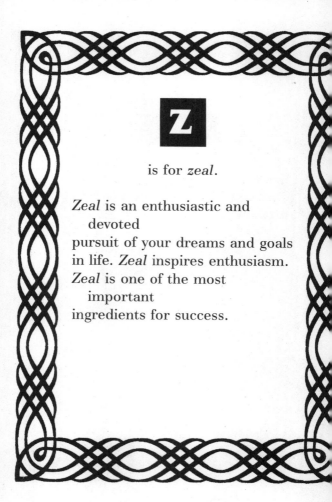

Z

is for *zeal*.

Zeal is an enthusiastic and
     devoted
pursuit of your dreams and goals
in life. *Zeal* inspires enthusiasm.
Zeal is one of the most
     important
ingredients for success.

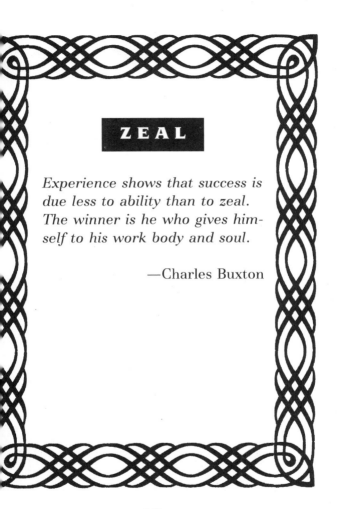

ZEAL

Experience shows that success is due less to ability than to zeal. The winner is he who gives himself to his work body and soul.

—Charles Buxton

The ABCs of Self-Esteem Activity Guide

The ABCs of Self-Esteem was designed to teach positive self-concepts and character ethos using a weekly mnemonics theme approach. Language arts skills are also advanced through communications and written assignments.

Things You Will Need

- Index cards

- Paper
- Pencils
- Glue
- Safety scissors
- Tape recorder (optional)

Activity: Select a theme; for example, "A is for attitude." Read the theme and the accompanying quotation.

Skills developed: Reading/self-esteem

Comments: Reading to their children is one of the most important things parents can do to help their children learn. Read the theme, related information, and quotation, and allow your children to read along with you. For older children let them read the theme, related information, and quotation to you. If you have a tape recorder, record the theme and quotation and play it back. Young children can repeat the theme after they hear the recording.

Activity: Discuss the theme and quotation.
Skills developed: Critical thinking/reading comprehension/listening/self-esteem
Comments: Children learn more when themes, concepts, words, and morals are discussed and they are allowed to participate in thought-provoking conversations.

Activity: Write and repeat the theme.

Skills developed: Vocabulary/ writing/self-esteem

Comments: When children say and write a word it helps them to comprehend it and make a permanent association with the word. Thus, the word easily becomes a part of their memory bank and vocabulary.

Activity: Repeat the theme; spell the theme; repeat the theme.

Skills developed: Speaking/spelling/self-esteem

Comments: Children who are good speakers and spellers become excellent readers. Excellent

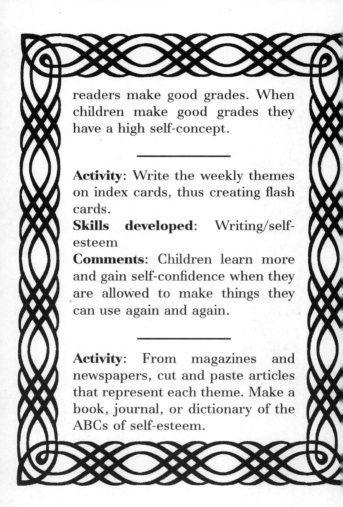

readers make good grades. When children make good grades they have a high self-concept.

Activity: Write the weekly themes on index cards, thus creating flash cards.

Skills developed: Writing/self-esteem

Comments: Children learn more and gain self-confidence when they are allowed to make things they can use again and again.

Activity: From magazines and newspapers, cut and paste articles that represent each theme. Make a book, journal, or dictionary of the ABCs of self-esteem.

Skills developed: Imagination/creativity/reading comprehension/self-esteem

Comments: Children will develop joy for a project when they are allowed to participate in it, and create something they can use. When learning is fun, children learn more.

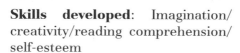

Activity: Tell your children a family story using one of the themes. For example, select a theme such as courage, faith, hope, persistence, or success.

Skills developed: Listening/cultural values/self-esteem

Comments: When children hear stories involving their family members, the concepts being taught at home become real and relevant. Children will want to learn the themes. Doing so bonds the children into their family and builds self-esteem.

Activity: Visit the library and help each of your children obtain a library card. Then check out and read books that tell the story of one of the themes. For instance, people with great courage and faith include Dr. Martin Luther King Jr., Harriet Tubman, and Helen Keller. Seek out their biographies and autobiographies.

Skills developed: Reading/listening/responsibility/self-esteem

Comments: Parents can encourage their children to read by modeling good reading habits and providing an environment that encourages reading. Schedule quiet time in the home—with no TV. Build a library or reading center in the home. When children read often, and are read to, they become better readers.

Activity: As a family watch a television show or rent a videotape that tells the story of one of the themes. Look for an example of great courage, faith, compassion, and hope. Discuss the theme, plot, and message.

Skills developed: Listening/verbal skills/appropriate television viewing habits

Comments: Television and other electronic media can have a positive influence on children if parents limit the amount of time their children watch TV and if parents supervise the programs their children watch. Educational and informational programs can increase children's understanding and knowledge of the environment and how it works. Television can stimulate children's imaginations and their zest for learning. Watching too much television, especially inappropriate programming can damage children's learning abilities.

Plan Your Own Activity

Planned Activity:

Skills Developed:

Comments:

Plan Your Own Activity

Planned Activity:

Skills Developed:

Comments:

Plan Your Own Activity

Planned Activity:

Skills Developed:

Comments:

Book Order Information

Please send me _____ copies of *The ABCs of Self-Esteem*, price $9.95

Please send me _____ copies of *Success Guideposts for African-American Children*, price $24.95

_____

Name (Please print)

_____

Telephone   Telephone (business)

_____

Address

_____ _____ _____

City   State   Zip

Shipping and handling add $3.95 for first book and $1.00 for each additional book. Illinois residents add 8.75% sales tax.

Send check or money order to:
W.Whorton & Company
P.O. Box 17787
Chicago, IL 60617
773-721-7500 or 800-649-7670
Fax Orders: 773-721-7560

Book Order Information

Please send me _____ copies of *The ABCs of Self-Esteem*, price $9.95

Please send me _____ copies of *Success Guideposts for African-American Children*, price $24.95

Shipping and handling add $3.95 for first book and $1.00 for each additional book. Illinois residents add 8.75% sales tax.

_____ Visa   _____ Master Card

_____ Discover   _____ American Express

Card number: _____

Name on card _____

_____
Address

_____ _____ _____
City   State   Zip

Telephone number: _____

Expiration date: _____/_____

Seminars/Workshops/ Educational Products Information

For additional information on educational products, books, tapes, seminars, workshops and lec-
tures by Will Horton, call toll free 800-649-7670
or send in the coupon below.

_____

Name (Please print)

_____

Address

_____   _____   _____

City   State   Zip

Please send information on ___Seminars
___Lectures ___Workshops ___ Books ___ Tapes
___ Educational products

Return to:
W.Whorton & Company
P.O. Box 17787
Chicago, IL 60617
773-721-7500 or 800-649-7670
Fax requests 773-721-7560

About the Author

Will Horton is an educator and educational consultant with 20 years of educational experience from early childhood to the college level. He is president of W. Whorton & Company, an educational publishing and consulting company. He provides workshops, seminars, and specialized training programs in a variety of topics for parents, schools, government institutions, and businesses. He is also the author of *Success Guideposts for African-American Children*.

How to Contact
Will Horton

E-mail:

Will.horton@gte.net

Write to:

Will Horton
P.O. Box 17787
Chicago, IL 60617

Library of Congress Cataloging in Publication Data

Horton, Will.
The ABCs of Self-Esteem: A simple A–Z Approach
to Building Self-Esteem Skills and Positive Character
Traits / Will Horton

    P.   CM.
 ISBN: 1-892274-16-7
 1. Self-Esteem 2. Character I. Title
 Library of Congress Catalog Card Number:
 98-96482